TROPICAL FISH
LOOK-AND-LEARN

by

MARY E. SWEENEY

Photographs: Dr. Herbert R. Axelrod, B. A. Branson, K. L. Chew, D. Conkel, J. Elias, S. Franke, Gan Fish Farm, R. Goldstein, H. Grier, B. Kahl, E. Kennedy, A. Kochetov, H. Linke, H. Mayland, A. Norman, J.Palicka, R. Pethiyagoda, MP & C. Piednoir, H.-J. Richter, A. Roth, S. Sane, W. Sommer, M. Smith, E. Taylor, K. Tanaka, J. Vierke, World Wide Fish Farm, M. Yamamoto, L. W. Yat, R. Zukal

Distributed in the UNITED STATES to the Pet Trade by T.F.H. Publications, Inc., One T.F.H. Plaza, Neptune City, NJ 07753; distributed in the UNITED STATES to the Bookstore and Library Trade by National Book Network, Inc. 4720 Boston Way, Lanham MD 20706; in CANADA to the Pet Trade by H & L Pet Supplies Inc., 27 Kingston Crescent, Kitchener, Ontario N2B 2T6; Rolf C. Hagen Ltd., 3225 Sartelon Street, Montreal 382 Quebec; in CANADA to the Book Trade by Macmillan of Canada (A Division of Canada Publishing Corporation), 164 Commander Boulevard, Agincourt, Ontario M1S 3C7; in the United Kingdom by T.F.H. Publications, PO Box 15, Waterlooville PO7 6BQ; in AUSTRALIA AND THE SOUTH PACIFIC by T.F.H. (Australia), Pty. Ltd., Box 149, Brookvale 2100 N.S.W., Australia; in NEW ZEALAND by Brooklands Aquarium Ltd. 5 McGiven Drive, New Plymouth, RD1 New Zealand; in Japan by T.F.H. Publications, Japan—Jiro Tsuda, 10-12-3 Ohjidai, Sakura, Chiba 285, Japan; in SOUTH AFRICA by Multipet Pty. Ltd., P.O. Box 35347, Northway, 4065, South Africa. Published by T.F.H. Publications, Inc.
Manufactured in the United States of America by T.F.H. Publications, Inc.

SUGGESTED READING

YF-100, 32 pages

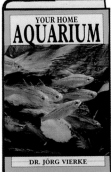

TS-139, 144 pages
Over 240 color photos

H-946, 320 pages
188 color photos

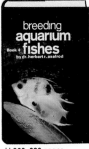

H-963, 320 pages
161 color photos

H-966, 448 pages
244 color photos

CO-002S, 128 pages
88 color photos

CO-003S, 128 pages
83 color photos

SK-033, 64 pages
Over 50 color photos

TU-016, 64 pages
93 color photos

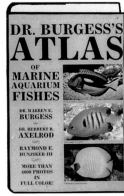

H-1077, over 1150 pages
Over 7000 color photos

H-1100, 736 pages
Over 4000 color photos

TS-104, 192 pages

E-701, 32 pages
20 color photos

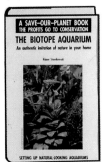

TT-026, 208 pages
Over 200 color photos

CO-007S, 128 pages
180 color photos

H-1097, 800 pages
Over 1700 color photos

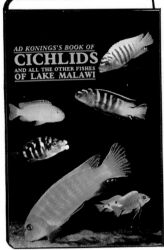

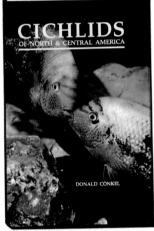

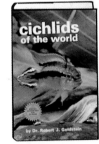

INTRODUCTION

When you start your first aquarium and find that you can keep beautifully colored tropical fishes happy and healthy, you have started a journey, the rewards of which cannot be measured by any standard yardstick. This is a hobby that will give you countless hours filled with fascinating observations. You will find that your imagination and your aquarium will take you to warm and wonderful places all over the globe as you learn more about your fishes, their habits, behaviors, and natural habitats. You will have the opportunity to observe firsthand a genuine miracle when your fishes present you with tiny fry. Most of all, if you haven't met him already, you will discover the natural scientist within yourself—the aquarist.

It is not difficult to set up an aquarium. Your pet shop has everything you need to get started—books, starter kits, tanks, filters, heaters...fishes. Just about all you have to do is add water. The most important

◄ Power filters are excellent for keeping your water in pristine condition. In addition to scouring the water of floating particles, the biological activity in the chamber will cleanse the water of toxic wastes. Photo courtesy of Hagen.

For the beginner, a quality starter kit includes all the necessary equipment. Photo courtesy of Hagen. ►

elements in tropical fishkeeping are the water, heater, filter, and tank. If kept in good, clean water of the right temperature and chemistry, most fishes will thrive (provided they have good food). The filter and regular water changes will keep the water fresh and sweet. The heater will keep the water the right temperature for tropicals. The tank, of course, will contain the clean, warmed water that will contain the fishes.

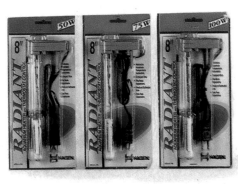

▲ All tropical aquaria require heaters. Even if you live in a warm climate, cool nights could lead to chilling of the fishes. Photo courtesy of Hagen.

▶

The scope and variety of aquarium products is awesome. There is no reason that everyone can't have the aquarium of their dreams. Photo courtesy of Hagen.

5

Wet-dry filtration is used with tremendous success in the saltwater side of the hobby. Units are now becoming available for the freshwater hobbyist as well. Photo courtesy of Hagen. ▶

There are air pumps for every purpose under water. No matter what type of filtration you use, you will find that an air pump will be handy to have. You can use them with extra filters and aerators. You never know when you are going to need extra air for your fishes. Photo courtesy of Hagen. ▼

Accessories like lights and hoods are useful...the hoods keep jumping fish from jumping out and the lights are handy for viewing fishes and necessary for growing plants.

As you grow with your aquarium, you will naturally want to customize it to your personal taste. Each person has their own interpretation of how an

◀ A thermometer is an essential piece of equipment. Your finger is just not accurate enough to gauge the temperature of the water for tropical fishes. Photo courtesy of Hagen.

▲ A "species tank" that contains only one kind of fish can be delightful. This gives the aquarist the opportunity to study the chosen species in great detail.

aquarium should look, and even using the same plants, rocks, driftwood, and decorations, no two aquaria ever look exactly the same.

When selecting your fishes, bear in mind that they will probably be youngsters that will grow quickly. If you are careful not to overstock the tank, your fishes and your filter will both have an opportunity to mature. If, like so many of us, you buy every fish you like, you will probably suffer heavy losses until the tank stabilizes. A good aquarium book like *Tropical Fish as a Hobby* (TFH TT-017) will give you step-by-step instructions on everything you need to know to get started.

▲ Nitrifying bacteria from a bottle will help get your aquarium filtering system up and running at peak efficiency in the least possible amount of time. Photo courtesy of Hagen.

▲ Internal power filters can be an excellent choice, especially when you don't have a lot of room for an outside filter. They are attractive and functional. Photo courtesy of Hagen.

A gravel washer is a wonderful ▶ device that cleans your gravel and removes the dirty water at the same time. Photo courtesy of Hagen.

AMAZING ANABANTOIDS

Anabantoids are generally gentle fishes—except for some rivalry between males—and on the whole are very amenable, excellent members of a peaceful community aquarium. They love warm water and will show their finest colors and manners when kept at around 80°F. Filtration of their water is not strictly necessary, but if you have a tendency to overstock or overfeed the tank, it is best to use a filter to make sure the water is kept clean. They do not like strong currents and soon become exhausted if they are not able to escape into calmer water. Plants are abundant in their native Asian waters and an important item in the anabantoid aquarium. The pH and hardness of the water is not important, but aged water is. This means that you should take care to change only very small amounts of water in an established aquarium.

Anabantoids have small, upturned mouths. They like all manner of small insects and worms, preferably floating on the top of the water or on the leaves of plants. They will feast on brine shrimp, tubifex, whiteworms, and bloodworms, but will readily accept prepared aquarium foods for their staple diet. Variety is very important, as is restraint from overfeeding.

◀A male Betta meets another male Betta with a great show of fins and flaring of gills—even when it's only his own reflection in the glass.

▶

Betta splendens, wild type. This is what the "real" Betta looks like. Is it any wonder that the Betta is one of the most popular of aquarium fishes?

▲ Female
Bettas display neither the color nor the finnage of their mates; however, they don't display their bad tempers either, and may be kept together in groups.

▶
Selective breeding has resulted in some unbelievable colors and fins on male Bettas. These fine fins, however, are very delicate and Bettas must not be subjected to nippy tankmates.

▲ One male Betta such as this is a splendid pet for a small aquarium. Given a small tank, a few plants, and a female, he will display for you his beautiful courtship ritual, bubblenest-building, spawning act, and fry care.

▶
Bettas will develop to their fullest potential if fed well on live foods and kept in clean, warm water.

▲ The Claret Betta (*Betta coccina*) is one of the beautiful bubblenest builders that the anabantoid enthusiast can add to his collection. During breeding, the colors intensify remarkably, making this peaceful species well worth a place in the aquarium.

Most anabantoids are bubblenest builders. The male blows bubbles of air and "spit," creating a nest that holds together very well in the still waters preferred by anabantoids. After the spawning act is completed, the male will tend the eggs in the bubblenest, constantly working around the nest and blowing ever more bubbles until the eggs begin to hatch into wrigglers. As the tiny fry fall out of the nest, the male tenderly picks them up in his mouth and returns them to the nest until they are free swimming.

▲ The Kalimantan Betta (*Betta foerschi*). With bubblenest builders, the male wraps his body around the female and fertilizes the eggs as she releases them.

The Striped Betta (*Betta fasciata*) explodes with blue iridescence during courtship and breeding.
▶

The Croaking Gourami (*Trichopsis vittatus*) blows bubbles to make its nest. When the fish spawn, the eggs float up into the bubblenest where they are tended by the male for the 36-hour incubation period. ▶

▲ The Crescent Betta (*Betta imbellis*) is fond of heavily planted tanks and will show its best colors and behavior in such a tank. This is a relatively peaceful Betta and can be kept easily in a community arrangement.

▲ The Paradisefish (*Macropodus opercularis*) was one of the first tropical fishes ever kept in the aquarium. It was imported to France from China in 1869 and was an immediate hit. Both males and females are quite aggressive; however, their good looks still make them desirable aquarium fish.

The Brunei Beauty (*Betta macrostoma*) is a mouthbrooder and the *male* carries the ▼ eggs!

11

Anabantoids are also called labyrinthfishes. The labyrinth is a special organ that allows them to breathe air from the surface of the oxygen-poor waters of their Asian homelands. This ability is a distinct advantage in nature, where they are found in shallow ditches, rice paddies, stagnant pools...wherever.

The labyrinth organ is very sensitive to chilling when it is developing in the fry and they should be kept in warm, covered tanks.

▲ The Honey Gourami (*Colisa chuna*) sports a dark blue to black throat that intensifies during courtship. They are very peaceful and shy and really appreciate a sunny, planted tank with quiet water.

◄ The Giant Gourami (*Colisa fasciata*) is not really all that big at 4 to 5 inches. Give them a warm, well-planted tank that is not disturbed often and they will surprise you with the number of fry they produce! They are a little shy when first brought home, but will become very lively as they adjust to the new conditions.

▶

The Three-Spot Gourami (*Trichogaster trichopterus*) in its gold form. The more common blue morph is an exceptionally beautiful two-toned navy and light blue fish. This is a lively, richly colored fish that is gregarious and very easily bred. The males are slightly territorial at breeding time, but only to repel invaders. Provide a warm, planted tank and good food and soon you will have several generations coexisting in harmony.

The Pearl Gourami (*Trichogaster leeri*) builds a bubblenest among the fine-leaved plants floating at the water's surface. Both the males and females are beautifully colored with red, silver, and blue. This is an easy fish to keep provided it is gently handled and well fed. Some fine-leaved plants, a little warmth, some peaceful tankmates, and you will find the Pearl Gourami blossoming into a lively, inquisitive fish. ▲

◀ Dwarf Gouramis are small, about 2 to 3 inches. The males are most colorful. The females are somewhat paler with more rounded fins. There are several color varieties and even long-finned types.

▲ The Chocolate Gourami (*Sphaerichthys osphromenoides*) is one of the mouthbrooding species of anabantoid. It will do very well in the aquarium provided there is adequate heat. Chilling is disastrous so keep the water at about 82°F for best results.

◀

The Dwarf Gourami (*Colisa lalia*) is one of the greatest aquarium fish going...hardy, easy to feed, peaceful, and gorgeous!

COOL CATFISHES

The miniature catfishes of the *Corydoras*, *Brochis*, and *Aspidoras* genera are the adorables of the aquarium with their delicate whiskers, saucy little winks, and generally comical demeanor. They have very easygoing personalities and are flexible about aquarium conditions. Relying on their sensitive barbels to locate their food, Corys spend most of their time "whiskering" every part of the aquarium. They are hungry little fellows and need to be kept well fed to maintain good condition.

Corydoras barbatus is an unusual species, one of the prettiest and largest of the Corys. Mature males sometimes develop bristles on their heads. ▶

Aspidoras pauciradiatus is a peaceful schooling species that is suitable for species tanks or community tanks with "safe" fishes. *Aspidoras* species appreciate small live foods in addition to their regular diet. ▶

◀ There have been no reported spawnings of *Corydoras axelrodi* in the aquarium. Be the first and become a part of aquarium history.

Corydoras panda was named after the popular Chinese panda "bear" for the black eye stripe. Among the most popular of the Corys, Pandas like good clean water and the company of their fellows.

▲ *Corydoras ambiacus* is a native of Peru and a friendly species that does best in small groups. They prefer extremely soft water and a dark sand substrate.

◄ *Corydoras guapore* was first collected by the famous explorer Harald Schultz. It is an active, nimble fish in the aquarium and should have enough open swimming space.

▲ *Corydoras aeneus* is very easy to keep and breed. They come from shallow waters with low oxygen content. Because of this, they sometimes rely on intestinal respiration and can be seen dashing to the surface for a mouthful of air. Aeneus is the most popular of all the Corys in the aquarium hobby.

Brochis britskii is a prize for any aquarist. The iridescent green and orangish coloration and large body size makes this an outstanding fish. ▲

Loricariids, or suckermouth catfishes, are found in a wide variety of habitats ranging from soft, acidic water in marshes to fast-moving mountain creeks. They like to stay near the banks and sometimes dig little caves in the muddy banks. Most Loricariid species are nocturnal and spend their nights roaming in search of food.

► Unusual catfishes like this *Pseudacanthicus* sp. are often imported from South America and kept in aquaria, but little is known about them from a scientific standpoint.

▲ *Hypostomus* sp., or Plecos, need plenty of vegetables in their diets. Vegetable-based flake foods, boiled and raw spinach, parboiled zucchini, boiled oatmeal, even rabbit pellets will satisfy these requirements.

▼ The genus *Pterygoplichthys* contains about 20 species coming mostly from Paraguay, Brazil, and Peru. Loricariids are highly territorial amongst themselves, but very peaceful with other fishes.

◀ The Panaque is a striking fish that is best suited to a large aquarium. It is highly nocturnal but as it becomes acclimated to aquarium life will make its presence known in the daytime.

▲ *Hypancistrus zebra* is the hottest new catfish to appear on the scene in a long time. A small fish that measures about four inches, it is also a little toughie that protects its chosen space with steadfast determination. The black and white pattern varies on different individuals.

▲ *Pseudacanthicus spinosus.* Suckermouth catfishes like to "chew" on driftwood. If you have a piece of driftwood and a suckermouth, you will invariably find little bits of sawdust around the tank from the fish's work. It is thought that they need the cellulose in the wood for digestion.

▲ *Ancistrus* are also known as Bristle-Nose Catfishes and have generally the same keeping requirements as the rest of the Loricariids. The bristles are present in both sexes, but more developed in the males, especially at breeding time. The bristles (sometimes called tentacles) are thought to be used to sense the speed and direction of the current of the water.

◀ A Panaque is a highly territorial fish and if it chooses the underside of a piece of driftwood as its home, that is where it will always return. Consider yourself lucky if its chosen locale can be observed during the daytime.

Catfishes have always been popular in the aquarium, but when one thought of catfishes, they usually pictured Corys and Plecos. Recently there has been a tremendous explosion in catfish species imported, everything from African upside-down catfishes (*Synodontis* spp.) to the Chacas of India and S.E. Asia to the Electric Catfish of Africa. There are enough different kinds of catfishes keep things interesting for a long time to come.

▲ The Angelicus Cat (*Synodontis angelicus*) is a rare, special catfish. As is so often the case with rarity, it is extremely beautiful as well. The Angelicus Cat is a nocturnal fish that hides in the mud during the day and comes out to feed only at night. It is very choosy about where it feeds, and is attracted to places with a lot of iron.

▶ The Chaca (*Chaca chaca*) is a sedentary, nocturnal catfish that likes to hang around the bottom of a well-planted aquarium. It is a very unusual-looking fish with its tough, lumpy skin, numerous barbels, huge mouth, and odd shape.

The mouth of the Chaca should alert you to the size of its appetite. Do not keep a Chaca with *any* fish smaller than its mouth! Even though the Chaca is a slow, "lazy" fish that is unlikely to be able to win in a chase-and-capture situation, it will sneak up on its prey when it's sleeping and... SNAP!

◀

◄*Agamyxis pectifrons* is one of those bizarre-looking talking catfishes. Doradids, or croaking catfishes, can make quite a din when alarmed. Many catfishes make sounds, and the doradids do this by rotation of the pectoral spines and resonation of the swimbladder.

The Electric Catfish (*Malapterurus electricus*) is a true novelty fish. The most interesting point about the fish is its ability to discharge electrical current that is used to deter predators and can perhaps be used to stun prey. Discharges have been measured between 100 and 450 volts, enough to knock a man down. ▲

◄ The Cuckoo Catfish (*Synodontis multipunctatus*) has cleverly devised a way to produce fry without any work. The female destroys the eggs and young of mouthbrooding cichlids and replaces them with her own to be reared.

Pimelodids have tremendously long whiskers that are sensory organs used for feeding and navigation in murky waters. They are somewhat soft-bodied compared to many of the other catfishes and rely on speed rather than armor as their defense. They are best kept in neutral to slightly acid water conditions in the 75 to 82°F. temperature range. ▼

▲ The Painted Talking Catfish (*Acanthodoras cataphractus*) is a native of the Middle Amazon region. It is relatively peaceful, nocturnal, and safe around any fish it cannot swallow. Be careful when handling this fish, however, as the first spine of the dorsal and pectoral fins is very stiff and sharp and can inflict a serious wound.

CHARMING CHARACOIDS

The group of fishes called characoids contains some unlikely bedfellows—Piranhas, Pencilfishes, Tetras, etc. —that have for scientific reasons landed in the same group. You might wonder what a Piranha has in common with a Cardinal Tetra, but if you were a scientist and looked at the anatomy of both, you would find that indeed they share common ancestors. The different (and similar) ways that each has evolved physically and adapted behaviorally are all part of a giant puzzle of life...past, present, and future.

Legends (and thriller movies) are made from such fish as the Dusky Piranha (*Serrasalmus calmoni*). These fish have a powerful instinct to turn upon and destroy anything that has been injured, even one of their own kind. ▶

▲ The Black Tetra (*Gymnocorymbus ternetzi*) is a hardy and undemanding species that can be a real beauty in the community aquarium. It is a fast fish that will indulge in fin-nipping, but cannot do any real damage to fishes larger than itself.

▼ The Rosy Tetra (*Hyphessobrycon bentosi*) is a very attractive fish that will show its best colors when kept in schools. A group of Rosy Tetras in a tank with a dark background and a little light from the front is a beautiful sight.

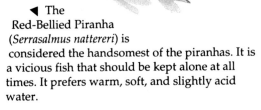

◀ The Red-Bellied Piranha (*Serrasalmus nattereri*) is considered the handsomest of the piranhas. It is a vicious fish that should be kept alone at all times. It prefers warm, soft, and slightly acid water.

▼ The Yellow-Tail African Characin (*Hemigrammopetersius caudalis*) is a native of the Congo River and its tributaries. Like so many characoids, they are jumpers and must be kept in a well-covered aquarium.

▲ The Splash Tetra (*Copella arnoldi*) has one of the strangest spawning rituals in the piscine world. The pair leap out of the water *together* and deposit their eggs on an overhanging leaf. The male stays under the leaf, splashing water on the eggs until they hatch three days later.

◀ The Red Phantom Tetra (*Megalamphodus sweglesi*) is happiest when kept in schools of six or more. They tend to be a little nippy, so choose their tankmates carefully. Avoid keeping them with fishes that have long, flowing fins. Feeding them small live foods will bring out their best colors.

▶ Keep your tank covered if you have the Marbled Hatchetfish (*Carnegiella strigata*)! They will take off and fly after their favorite foods, flying insects.

◀ The Striped Headstander (*Anostomus anostomus*) swims in a head-down position, constantly checking the bottom for food. They are peaceful fish that like large, well-planted aquaria.

◀ The Mexican Tetra (*Astanyx fasciatus*) is the only characin that is found in the United States. They are best kept in slightly alkaline water of about 70 to 75°F. Supply some vegetables in the diet.

All characoids are egglayers that spray their eggs wherever there is a handy thicket of plants. In nature their spawning and the rainy season coincide, but in the aquarium they will spawn year-round. Generally the males have longer dorsal and anal fins and brighter colors; the females are usually stouter through the middle than the males.

▶ The Six-Lined Distichodus (*Distichodus sexfasciatus*) is a large, good-looking fish that needs a large tank and plenty of greens in its diet. Neutral to slightly acid, warm water and peaceful tankmates are appreciated.

◀ Congo Tetras (*Phenacogrammus interruptus*) are beautiful in the sunlight or soft fluorescent lighting. Bright incandescent lighting washes out their colors. Their iridescence comes from the prismatic effect of the guanine in the large scales.

▲ The African
Characidium (*Nannocharax fasciatus*) has
a habit of sitting up on its pectoral fins,
somewhat like a goby. It is a peaceful,
small fish about three inches long that
likes a quiet tank and plenty of live
worms.

◄ The Redhook Metynnis (*Myleus rubripinnis*)
is peaceful and shy and happiest in groups of its own
kind. It is very fond of plants and will destroy a
planted tank in no time. Offer some
good vegetable foods. It won't save
your plants, but your Redhook
will be happy.

◄ The Cardinal Tetra
(*Paracheirodon axelrodi*) is the
ultimate schooling fish. The bigger
the school, the happier they are and
the more beautiful the display. To
keep your Cardinals happy, give them
soft, acidic, warm water. They are not
fussy eaters, but foods must be small enough
for them to fit in their small mouths.

► The Silver-Tipped
Tetra (*Hasemania nana*) is a very
peaceful schooling fish that
should be kept with at least six
of its own kind. It needs slightly
acid, soft water. It comes from
southeastern Brazil.

◄ The Emperor Tetra (*Nematobrycon
palmeri*) is one of the prettiest of
the South American tetras
and very easy to keep. Give it
clean, soft, slightly acid
water and a peaceful tank.
Emperor Tetras are easy to feed
and will take flake with just as much
gusto as the tastiest live foods.

A a characoid is a very fish-like fish. It is usually greater in depth than in thickness and has a streamlined appearance. All of them have teeth and scales and none of them have whiskers. Many of them have an extra fin called an adipose fin on the top rear of their bodies.

▲ The Banded Leporinus (*Leporinus nigrofasciatus*) grazes constantly on algae that covers plant surfaces. Once the algae is gone, they will turn their attention to the tender young leaves of the plants. It helps to add some vegetables to their diets.

▼ Yellow-Banded Moenkhausia (*Moenkhausia sanctaefilomenae*) is a very active, omnivorous fish that is easy to keep. It will leave your plants alone if you give it some vegetables in its diet. They are easy to breed, needing only a thicket of plants and a pair of fish.

▼ The Buenos Aires Tetra (*Hemigrammus caudovittatus*) is a very attractive, highly iridescent, perky little fish. It likes the company of its fellows and should have a well-covered tank. Tetras are leapers and will escape to their dooms through openings in the tank cover.

▼ The Red-Spotted Copeina (*Copeina guttata*). This fish is a characin, but seems to think its a cichlid at spawning time. The male scoops out a depression in the gravel in which the female lays a large number of eggs. The eggs are then fanned and guarded by the male.

The Brown-Tailed Pencilfish (*Nannostomus eques*) is a peaceful fish that prefers to swim with its head tilted upward in small schools. The male is much slimmer and more colorful than the female.

▶

▼ Beckford's Pencilfish (*Nannostomus beckfordi*). Most of the pencilfishes have an odd characteristic. At night, their body markings change drastically. This species loses its stripes and develops large spots.

▼ The Red-Eyed Characin (*Arnoldichthys spilopterus*) is one of the most common African tetras. It is highly iridescent and reflects all the colors of the rainbow. This species is sensitive to changes in water conditions, so you should make only small water changes at any given time.

▶ The Black-Finned Colossoma (*Colossoma macropomum*) is a close relative of the piranha and displays something of its nasty temperament. This is a big fish that needs a big aquarium.

CAPTIVATING CICHLIDS

Cichlids have earned a solid position in the hearts and tanks of tropical fish hobbyists. They are generally very hardy, easy to sex and breed, very colorful, and interesting, with many of them becoming tame enough to take food from their owner's fingers. They can also be feisty, territorial, and tough, but cichlid enthusiasts soon learn how to deal with their peculiarities, be it by increasing the tank size, creating artificial boundaries in the aquarium, or selecting more suitable tankmates (or none at all!).

▶ An albino form of the Oscar (*Astronotus ocellatus*). Oscars are great pets and will certainly become very tame with a little attention from their owners.

The Convict Cichlid (*Heros nigrofasciatus*) is one of the easiest of all aquarium fishes to breed. These prolific and devoted parents will herd their young into pits they have dug in the substrate for protection.

▼

The Oscar is not only a real "personality," but a chowhound as well. To keep Oscar happy, you must be prepared to give him meaty, chunky foods. Oscars are messy eaters, so plan accordingly when setting up your filtration.

◀ The Pearlscale Cichlid (*Herichthys carpinte*), like most largish cichlids, makes a real mess in a decorated aquarium. Forget about plants and cute little ornaments. Big, clunky rocks and hefty pieces of driftwood are the way to go.

The Spilotum (*Herichthys nicaraguense*) is unusual in that after egglaying, the parents move the eggs and combine them with the eggs and fry of other females. Then all the adults in the group protect the eggs and young. ▼

◀ The Green and Gold Cichlid (*Herichthys lentiginosus*). The fish in this photo fish is silvery-blue because he's in breeding coloration. An 8-inch vegetarian in its native Guatemala, it will do quite well in the aquarium with vegetable-based pellets.

The Red-Spot Cichlid (*Herichthys bifasciatus*) grows to about one foot in length and likes vegetables and algae. It will eat meaty foods in the aquarium, but won't molest smaller fishes unless very, very hungry. ▼

◀The Severum (*Heros severus*) is found all over tropical South America and in many, many aquaria. Severums are quite gentle for large cichlids—until spawning time—and pairs will do well in a 40- or 50-gallon aquarium.

Cichlids come in all sizes and shapes, from the very, very big to the petite dwarf cichlids. Most cichlids are shaped, well, like fish, but if you look at the Discus and Angelfish, you will see that they are very high bodied and very narrow if you look at them head-on. Some cichlids have humps on their foreheads (cephalic humps) that are not, as many people would like to believe, a sign of brains, but rather a place where fat is stored. But if cichlids are known for anything, it's their fabulous coloration. Colors, the brightest, and outrageous patterns make the cichlids stand out among all the aquarium fishes.

The Blackbelt Cichlid (*Herichthys maculicauda*) is a big, beefy cichlid that is fond of green foods. Many people make the mistake of thinking that a big fish needs only meat; not true, most fishes need a balanced diet that includes greens.

The Jack Dempsey (*Herichthys octofasciatus*) has been an aquarium favorite for over 100 years. The highly iridescent spots on the body are beacons in its murky native waters. ▼

◀ The Cockatoo Cichlid (*Apistogramma cacatuoides*) is what is called a dwarf cichlid. They like a quiet life with other small, peaceful species.

▶

The Green Terror (*Aequidens rivulatus*) is large, aggressive, and gorgeous. Give them plenty of elbow room. Cichlids are "intelligent" fishes that soon learn how to interact with their keepers.

The Elusive Cichlid (*Acaricthys heckeli*) stymied fish breeders for many years until it was found that the males keep harems of females and spawn in protected areas like caves. Not exactly a likely scenario for the casual hobbyist.

◄ This pair of the beautiful Agassiz's Dwarf Cichlids (*Apistogramma agassizi*) clearly shows the long, fancier fins of the male. Females tend to be a little less splendid. The small female, however, will quickly beat the male if he is not removed from the area after the eggs have been fertilized.

▲ The Firemouth (*Herichthys meeki*) isn't meek at all. Endowed with a bright red throat and gill area, Firemouths flare their gills at the first sign of trouble. The large and fiery gills are usually enough to send troublemakers on their way.

► Another dwarf cichlid, the Ram (*Microgeophagus ramirezi*) is very timid and should be given a quiet, planted tank with aged water. Its beauty alone makes it worthy of its own private quarters.

Angelfish and Discus are both unique, but for opposite reasons. Angelfish (*Pterophyllum* species) started the love affair hobbyists have with cichlids and Discus (*Symphysodon* species) were shrouded in mystery and challenging to keep and breed.

This cobalt blue Discus clearly shows a bright red eye. The red eye is a most desirable trait in both Discus and Angelfish. ▲

◀ This is a Brown Discus (*S. aequifasciatus axelrodi*). The Brown Discus is considered "common," but it is the progenitor of many of the most beautiful Discus strains available today.

◀ Angelfish come in almost countless color varieties and fin types. The top fish is the wild-type Angel, from which all other varieties were developed. The lower fish is a black veiltail, one of the early developments in Angelfish breeding.

◄ The best conditions for Discus are soft, acid, warm, and clean water. There is no substitute for this if you want to have healthy, happy Discus.

► The wide bar in the center of the body of this fish indicates that it has some Heckel blood in its lineage. Selective breeding has produced Discus without *any* bars visible at all.

◄ The Silver Angel. This beautiful fish is peaceful, hardy, and will delight you with its good manners. Angels rarely cause trouble except when they are trying to breed and other fish interfere with them.

A very popular new strain of Discus called "Red Dragon." These fish are covered with a peppering of tiny black spots that concentrate around the face and fins. They are very hardy and easy to keep. ►

◄ The Discus hobby is still waiting for a pure red Discus. Pure blue Discus have been developed, but so far all the reds also have other colors on their bodies.

Africa, with its lakes, rivers, and streams, is home to many fascinating cichlid species. The rift lakes, Malawi and Tanganyika in particular, contain some very special cichlids that have adapted to the very hard, very alkaline waters found there. The riverine cichlids of Africa, however, are adapted to softer, more acidic water, and genuinely require these conditions for their well-being.

▶ The Blue Hap (*Copadichromis azureus*) is one of the haplochromine cichlids of Lake Malawi. These are schooling fish that primarily eat plankton, but adapt to aquarium life very easily.

▼ One of the glorious Peacocks (*Aulonocara stuartgranti*) of Lake Malawi. Among the most brightly colored of the rift lake fishes, they should be kept in hard, alkaline water with a temperature of about 80°F.

▼ The Kribs (*Pelvicachromis pulcher*) are among the best-loved of the African dwarf cichlids. Found in the rivers of tropical West Africa, Kribs do *best* if their water is about 80°F, soft, and slightly acid. When the females are filled with eggs, their little red bellies will become beacons to the males.

◄ An Orange Zebra (*Pseudotropheus zebra*). The teeth of these mbuna are almost like velcro, designed for scraping algae and small crustaceans off rocks.

▲ The Purple Mbuna (*Melanochromis vermivorous*) is as feisty and quarrelsome as it is beautiful. The social hierarchy demands that there is always a bully in the tank. If you remove the bully, the next most dominant fish will assume the role of the bully.

◄ Nichols's Mouthbrooder (*Pseudocrenilabrus nicholsi*) is from Zaire and much sought after by hobbyists for its stunning good looks and interesting mouthbrooding behavior.

Another beautiful Peacock (*Aulonocara baenschi*) from Lake Malawi. Peacocks are a bit less aggressive than mbuna, the other Lake Malawi rock-dwelling cichlids, so they may be a bit more desirable if you want a peaceful aquarium. ▶

◄ Blue Zebra (*Pseudotropheus zebra*). There are many, many different color morphs of Zebras. To keep the peace in an mbuna tank, it is necessary to provide an abundance of caves and other hiding places so they can establish their territories.

Most of the African cichlids are very aggressive and territorial—even more so than their South and Central American cousins. One way to defuse future battles is to make sure to create ample hiding places in the form of rockwork and driftwood when you are setting up your African cichlid tank. The dominant fish will stake out its territory, usually in the center of the tank, and the others will have smaller territories within the labyrinth of rocks and wood. Another way to dilute the aggressive behavior is by "controlled crowding," where you put about twice as many fish in the tank as you would normally. If you are going to try this technique, make sure you have ample hiding places, a great filter, and don't overfeed.

▲ Burton's Mouthbrooder (*Haplochromis burtoni*). An interesting feature in these fish is the presence of "egg spots" on the anal fin of the male. The female lays her eggs and picks them up in her mouth. As she tries to pick up the fake eggs on the male's anal fin, he releases his sperm and the eggs are fertilized in her mouth.

◀ The Frontosa (*Cyphotilapia frontosa*) is a native of Lake Tanganyika. The cephalic hump that makes them look so wise is largest in older males and absent, or nearly so, in females and juvenile males. These interesting fish come from deep waters but adapt to and even breed in a large aquarium.

▶

The Duboisi (*Tropheus duboisi*) lives among the algae-covered rocks in Lake Tanganyika. They are maternal mouthbrooders, but are difficult to breed in that the female lays very few eggs, about 6 to 12, and carries them for about four weeks.

◄ The male Yellow-Tipped Ventralis (*Ophthalmotilapia ventralis*) have very long pelvic fins with tassels on the ends. The females mouth these tassels to stimulate the male to fertilize the eggs they are carrying in their mouths.

Lake Tanganyika's Dickfeldi (*Julidochromis dickfeldi*) lays her eggs upside down on the roof of a cave and the male follows in the same upside down posture to fertilize them. ►

◄ The male Six-Bar Cichlids (*Lamprologus sexfasciatus*) "Gold" will stake out their territories in caves, from where they will emerge to grab live foods like brine shrimp, and frozen and flake foods. They, like most of the rift lake cichlids, should have foods with some vegetable content.

The Calvus (*Altolamprologus calvus*) from Lake Tanganyika is as fragile as it is beautiful. This is a very picky eater that will only take live foods, like adult brine shrimp and small fishes. It took years for them to be bred in captivity and if you can find and take care of one, it is a prize indeed. ▼

►

Ornatus (*Julidochromis ornatus*) are unusual for rift lake cichlids in that they are not mouthbrooders. Give them live foods like brine shrimp until they are settled in to the aquarium and then slowly wean them to prepared foods.

Cichlids have made some remarkable adaptations to their environments. Some of them are maternal mouthbrooders that pick up their eggs and carry them in the safety of their mouths until the fry are big enough to fend for themselves. Others spawn on a flat rock and both parents defend the eggs with their lives. Others spawn on the roofs of caves, and some even "nurse" their fry until they are old enough to eat larger foods. One thing almost every cichlid will do is guard their eggs and fry against every danger, even unto death.

Jewel Cichlids (*Hemichromis bimaculatus*) are famous for their parenting. These large, yellow eggs will be ferociously defended. When the fry are free-swimming, they will be herded around by their parents until they are old enough to fend for themselves.
▶

▲
Eartheaters (*Geophagus steindachneri*) lay their eggs "in typical cichlid fashion" and then fan them for a day or so. The eggs are then picked up in the mouth of one or both parents and incubated. Even after the fry are released, they are welcomed back (for a time) into the parent's mouth for security.

▶
The tiny free-swimming fry of this Orange Chromide (*Etroplus maculatus*) will grow quickly on a diet of newly hatched brine shrimp.

◄ This close-up shows the "eyed-up" fry in the buccal cavity of the mother. The mother does not usually eat when she is holding fry in her mouth.

▲ Discus are remarkable parents. The fry feed off the "Discus Milk" (actually body slime) of both parents, who shift the tiny school from one to the other as they tire of the duty.

After the male Egyptian Mouthbrooder (*Pseudocrenilabrus philander*) has fertilized the laid eggs, the female picks them up in her mouth where they incubate for about ten days. When the fry hatch, they are faithfully guarded by the mother. If danger threatens, she opens her big mouth and the babies all crowd in again like little sardines in a can. ▼

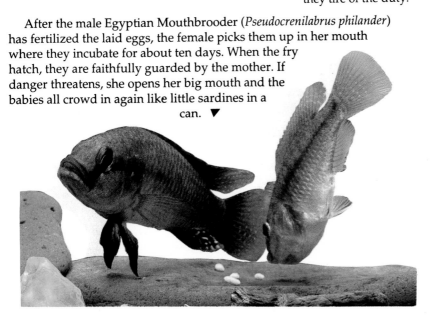

CYPRINID CIRCLE

Cyprinids, members of the family Cyprinidae, include many different types of fishes: Koi, Barbs, Danios, Rasboras, and Minnows. It is hard to imagine that they are all related—some are coldwater fishes and some are tropical fishes—but they are indeed related to each other as well as to the Catfishes and Tetras.

▼ The Clipper Barb (*Barbodes callipterus*) is a West African species that needs soft, slightly acid water but accepts a wide temperature range of 70 to 86°F. This is a challenging species to breed because it spawns under different water conditions at different times of the year.

▶ The Long-Finned Zebra Danio (*Brachydanio rerio*) is a peaceful, active fish that has long been the mainstay of the beginner's community tank. They are forgiving of many of the novice aquarist's mistakes, but do like their water clean and well-aerated. The long-finned variety gives the small fish a definite "presence" in the aquarium.

(*Barbodes candens*) is a fairly new species of African barb that joins the 300 or so other barbs native to "The Dark Continent." ▶

◀ The Checker Barb (*Capoeta oligolepis*) is hardy, peaceful, active, and easy to breed. If you want to breed egg-scatterers (as this type of egglayer is called), cover the bottom of the tank with large pebbles or marbles to protect the eggs and fry from being eaten by the parents.

◀ The Cherry Barb (*Puntius titteya*) is one of the best barbs for the community tank. It is peaceful and very colorful, in and out of spawning mode. They will take all aquarium foods but display a particular fondness for brine shrimp.

▲ The Clown Barb (*Barbodes everetti*) is a hardy, attractive fish that requires a large tank for its busy life. It should not be kept with smaller fishes for even though it is a dedicated plant eater, it is not above snapping up a small fish. These are not the easiest fish to spawn in the aquarium. The trick is to separate the sexes for three weeks before spawning.

▼ Leopard Danio (*Brachydanio frankei*). This is the long-finned form of a very attractive Danio that comes from India. A busy and active fish, it likes a clean, well-aerated tank with a little sunshine.

▲ The Asian Rummy-Nose (*Sawbwa resplendens*). The females are almost completely colorless, but the males show blood red on their noses and the tips of their tails. These fish are relatively new to the hobby and not yet easy to find in pet shops.

There are hundreds of species of cyprinids that are suitable for the home aquarium. The majority of them are natives of Southeast Asia, but are bred in great numbers on fish farms and can be found in almost every pet shop. They are easy to keep, hardy, active, and colorful. They are undemanding with regards to water chemistry, but for the most part prefer soft, acidic water conditions for breeding.

▲ The so-called "Moss Green" Tiger Barb (*Capoeta tetrazona*). Like the other color varieties, this is a hardy, easy-to-breed barb. The only drawback to breeding Tiger Barbs is that they will turn around and devour the eggs as soon as they have finished spawning. Protect the eggs with fine-leaved plants like Java Moss or a marble substrate and remove the parents when they have finished laying the eggs.

▶ The Tiger Barb (*Capoeta tetrazona*) is flashy, colorful, and active. This hardy fish is a great aquarium fish except for one little bad habit; it loves to nip the fins of its tankmates, the longer and fancier, the better. One way to keep this problem to a minimum is to keep your Tiger Barbs in a school. They will spend so much time "playing tag" with each other, they won't bother with the other fishes.

Wilpita (*Rasbora wilpita*). Rasboras are excellent aquarium fishes. They are the ideal size for almost any tank (1 to 5 inches), are extremely peaceful, hardy, and of outstanding beauty. They do well on flake food, but live foods are usually necessary to bring them into breeding condition. ▼

▲ The Rosy Barb (*Puntius conchonius*) is a very active, well-behaved fish but the temptation to nip the long fins of tankmates might prove overwhelming at times.

◄ The Black Spot Barb (*Puntius filamentosus*). When in breeding color, the males of this species are outstanding with their red fins, black stripes, and golden bodies. They are good jumpers and care should be taken to keep the tank well covered. A long, low tank is best for these active fish.

The Harlequin Rasbora (*Rasbora heteromorpha*) is a native of Malaysia and parts of Sumatra. They are peaceful, active fish that prefer to travel in schools. The Harlequin requires soft, acid water for breeding and this water is best for general keeping as well.
►

The Half-Striped Barb (*Capoeta semifasciolatus*) is a native of Southern China that likes a sunny aquarium and plenty of plants. This fish needs swimming space, so use at least a 20-gallon aquarium.
▼

◄ The White Cloud Mountain Minnow (*Tanichthys albonubes*) is an ideal aquarium fish! There's no fuss, no muss with White Clouds. Give them a tank and some water and they'll be happy. They need no heater, no special foods, just some clean, filtered water.

KILLIFISH CULTURE

Killifishes are small, very brightly colored annual fishes that have a life span of only about a year. Because they inhabit temporary bodies of water that dry up after nine months to a year, the pressure is on to mature and reproduce before the next dry season. With the coming of the next rainy season, the eggs that were laid in the mud hatch and the new generation of killies appears.

◀ The Lace-Finned Killie (*Pterolebias zonatus*) is one of the larger killies, measuring in at about 4 to 5 inches. Most killies are very small, usually less than three inches, but their colors make up for their short lives and diminutive size.

The Two-Striped Killie (*Aphyosemion bivittatum*). This beautiful killie likes a quiet tank that is well planted and not too brightly lit. Killies like well-aged acid water that is about 77°F.

▶

Rivulins like this *Rivulus igneus* are peaceful and shy with other fishes. Be sure to cover the tank very well, as they are known to be able to escape through tiny openings in the tank cover. ▲

The Striped Panchax (*Aplocheilus lineatus*) has a mouth that promises to devour smaller fishes kept in the same aquarium. Segregate these fish in a tank of their own or keep them with larger peaceful fishes that require the same neutral to slightly acidic water conditions. ▲

◀ The Peruvian Longfin (*Pterolebias peruensis*) spawns, like most killies, in soft, acidic water. Use a layer of peat moss about an inch deep on the bottom of the spawning aquarium and the fish will bury themselves in the moss as they lay their eggs.

◀ Rachow's Notho (*Nothobranchius rachovi*) is as quarrelsome as it is handsome. This calls for private quarters in a small tank with a few fish. The male drapes his dorsal fin over the back of the female during spawning.

The Sicklefin Killie (*Cynolebias dolichopterus*) is a two-inch long, timid Venezuelan native. Keep this little prize in a small show tank with neutral water and small live foods. ◀

▲ The Persian Minnows (*Aphanias mento*) are unusual for killies in that they prefer hard, alkaline water with about one teaspoon of salt per gallon. Live foods with some vegetable matter added will keep them in peak condition.

LOVELY LIVEBEARERS

Guppies, Mollies, Platies, and Swordtails are the "Big Four" of the aquarium hobby. It is the rare aquarist that has not kept at least one of the species at some time in his career. These fish are all livebearers, which means they do not lay eggs, but bear living young. This is tremendously fascinating in that you can see the babies being born and immediately swimming off to start their own lives.

▲ The Balloon Molly (*Poecilia sphenops* var.) is the ideal of beauty to some and to others an abomination. There are many outstanding varieties of livebearers that have been developed from rather plain looking wild stock.

▲ Hi-Fin Platy. Platies, Swordtails, Mollies, and Guppies have been bred for a number of special characteristics. Some have big dorsal fins, some have spectacular tails, intense coloration, or unusual color patterns.

▼ The Yucatan Sailfin Molly (*Poecilia velifera*) is a hard fish to beat for looks with its magnificent dorsal fin. Sailfin Mollies have somewhat more definite keeping requirements than the Guppies and Platies. Not all livebearers are easy fish to keep (even though many people seem to lump them together). Give your Sailfins hard, alkaline water in the 73-79°F temperature range and plenty of vegetable matter in their diets.

▲ The Platy (*Xiphophorus maculatus*) is peaceful, active, and an ideal community fish. Hardy in the extreme, Platies are able to take a pretty wide range of water conditions and still enjoy vitality and good health.

▶ The Guppy (*Poecilia reticulata*) is one fish that everyone knows. Known as the Millions Fish for years because they produced so many young, the Guppy has earned a solid position in the aquarium hobby. There are many, many varieties of Guppy with fantastic color, size, and shape.

◀

The male Guppy is the one with the brilliant colors. Females are fairly dull and olive-gray, sometimes with just a touch of color in their tails. Males are generally smaller through the body, but cultivated varieties more than make up for this with their tail and dorsal fin development.

The Swordtail (*Xiphophorus helleri*) is the largest of the commonly kept livebearers. Swordtails come in many different colors and patterns. They are among the prettiest of the aquarium fishes with the males sporting a swordlike extension on the tail. Large females can give birth to as many as 150 young every 30 days.

▼

◀ The Sailfin Molly (*Poecilia latipinna*) likes warm, slightly alkaline water with about one teaspoon of salt added per gallon. Mollies, and indeed most other livebearers, are primarily vegetarian and will constantly pick at live plants and algae in the aquarium.

To keep livebearers happy, just think of a summer vacation near the beach. They like clean, warm, and slightly salty water about 74 to 78° F. Add a few plants and some light, good food, and you have happy livebearers. Because most livebearers are fairly small, you can have a good community setup in a relatively small aquarium of 10 or 20 gallons. Start off with two or three pairs, and soon you will have a stable population that will continually replenish itself.

▲ This male Merry Widow approaches the female from slightly below and behind; 23 to 27 days later about 40 live young will be born.

▼ The Half-Beak (*Nomorhamphus celebensis*) is an Indonesian livebearer that must have live foods like brine shrimp or small Guppies to survive in the aquarium. They should be kept by themselves in a small planted tank.

▶ Sunburst Platies are very bright yellow and orangeish red. This attractive variety is very popular and the colors will be enriched by feedings of brine shrimp and plant material in the diet.

◄ The Four-Eyes (*Anableps anableps*) is a large fish and has eyes in elevated sockets that give it the ability to see in air as well as water.

Gold Dust Molly (*Poecilia sphenops*). Mollies are the least likely of the common livebearers to eat their babies. Keep all of your livebearers well fed and they will be less likely to eat the fry. Give livebearers well-planted tanks so the young can hide amongst the leaves of the plants. ►

◄ This is a male Salt-and-Pepper Platy. The entire body of the fish is covered with innumerable small black spots. Red strains of Platies need temperature in the upper ranges to hold their color well. Be sure to give these fish enough vegetable foods as these are color-enhancers as well.

▼ The Merry Widow (*Phallichthys amates*) is giving birth to its large fry. The fry is presenting tail first in this case. Most livebearer babies are curled up in a little ball when they are born and in seconds straighten out and swim away.

Gambusia (*Gambusia puncticulata*) is often used for mosquito control in small pools. Gambusia are intolerant of other fishes and will bully any fish that lets them get away with it. ▼

RAINBOW ROUNDUP

Rainbowfishes are natives of Australia and New Guinea. They are ideal aquarium fishes in that they are spectacular in their beauty, easygoing, and very hardy. They don't ask for much in the way of keeping and a 20-gallon tank will house three or four adults very comfortably. They are easily fed and will take flake food just as willingly as the choicest live foods.

Australia is very strict about import and export of animals, and the rainbowfishes we enjoy in the aquarium hobby are almost exclusively captive bred in the Far East rather than collected from the wild.

▲ The Eastern Rainbowfish (*Melanotaenia splendida splendida*) lives near the surface of small streams, lakes, and reservoirs, usually in great schools.

▶ The Goldie River Rainbow (*Melanotaenia goldiei*) is found in rainforest streams, usually near sunken logs. This indicates that these fish feel most comfortable with some cover so provide a piece of driftwood in the tank.

▼ The Banded Rainbowfish (*Melanotaenia trifasciata*) shows its most beautiful colors when it is in an aquarium that receives two or three hours of natural sunlight a day.

▶ The Splendid Rainbowfish (*Melanotaenia splendida rubrostriata*) is found in heavily vegetated areas at the margins of streams, lagoons, and shallow lakes. What this means for the fishkeeper is that they should be offered a planted tank.

◀ The Irianjaya Rainbowfish (*Melanotaenia irianjaya*). Rainbowfish need regular water changes or they will develop tuberculosis.

◀ The Red Rainbowfish (*Glossolepis incisus*) is from New Guinea. The male is gorgeous with his salmon-red coloration and the female is golden. They are schooling fish that because of their size require at least a 30-gallon tank to stretch their fins properly.

◀

The Lake Kutubu Rainbow (*Melanotaenia lacustris*). Rainbowfishes are known for their longevity with a usual life expectancy of about four to eight years.

▶

Boeseman's Rainbowfish (*Melanotaenia boesemani*) is a wonderfully handsome fish with its navy-blue front and golden-orange rear. This is an unusual distribution of color for a fish; usually if the colors vary, the darker color is on the top of the fish and the lighter color on the underside.

Rainbowfishes are non-pair bonding egg scatterers that can be bred in pairs, trios, or groups. It is best to keep different species of rainbows in separate tanks because if kept together they will interbreed with each other and hybrid fishes are not desirable.

The males' colors get very bright just prior to spawning, which is as good an indication as any that they are about to breed. After the eggs are laid, it is best to remove the spawning surface and let the eggs hatch in a separate tank. The eggs will hatch in 6 to 12 days. The fry are transparent and very small, but can generally be found just below the surface of the water. The fry must be fed very often (about every 2 hours) on powdered fry food and infusoria.

◀ The Fly River Rainbowfish (*Melanotaenia sexlineata*) is a native of the Fly River in Papua New Guinea. The hardest part of finding rainbowfishes in the wild is getting to and from their habitat. They are typically found in remote areas that barely have any roads at all.

The Sentanien Rainbow (*Melanotaenia* ▼ *sentaniensis*). Rainbows spawn in a manner similar to killifish. A pair will scatter eggs among fine-leaved plants like Java moss or a yarn mop. The eggs have adhesive threads that bind them to the moss or the fibers of the yarn.

▶ Parkinson's Rainbowfish (*Melanotaenia parkinsoni*) is a native of Papua New Guinea that prefers deep water with submerged driftwood.

◀ Papuan Rainbowfish (*Melanotaenia papuae*). Rainbowfishes, because of their predilection toward mosquito larvae, represent an excellent natural control for these insects.

▶ North New Guinea Rainbow (*Melanotaenia affinis*). Rainbowfishes are very peaceful except for occasional "renegades," large males that tend to bully smaller fish during spawning time. Add more females to distract the bully male and you will have peace once again.

Most rainbows are very active and quite fearless. This makes them good "dither fish" for shy cichlids. A dither fish is one that convinces, through its fearlessness, a shy fish to come out and show itself. Their speed is useful in keeping them from harm once the shy cichlid has decided not only to come out of hiding, but to take a nip out of its tankmates. Because of similar water requirements and speed, rainbows are one of the few kinds of fishes that make fine tankmates for rift lake cichlids.

▲
Spotted Blue-Eye (*Pseudomugil gertrudae*). The Spotted Blue-Eye is found in *billabongs*, or swampy marshes and other backwaters. They are fond of densely planted tanks with driftwood and plenty of algae.

▶ Featherfin Rainbow (*Iratherina werneri*). The Featherfin Rainbow is one of the smallest of the rainbows, measuring in at under two inches. It is, however, a pretty little thing with its long fins and forked tail. It is found in weed-choked, slow-moving waters and so should be given good cover in the aquarium.

Pacific Blue-Eye (*Pseudomugil signifer*). The spectacular finnage of this blue-eyed fish makes it a desirable addition to any rainbowfish collection! They almost look like they could take off and fly with their fluttering fins. Their small upturned mouths indicate that they are surface feeders and prefer tiny insects that land on the water's surface. ▶

◀ Forktail Rainbowfish (*Pseudomugil furcata*). A tank full of the small "Blue-Eyes" is an outstanding sight. Each of them has interesting finnage and beautiful coloration and they are so peaceful there's no need to be concerned about compatibility.

▼ Popondetta Rainbowfish (*Pseudomugil connieae*). Popondettas are from rainforest streams, frequently near rapids, where they live in schools of 30 or more. Their diet includes tiny insects taken from the surface of the water, small crustaceans, and some algae.

The Madagascar Rainbow (*Bedotia geayi*) is, as the common name suggests, a native of Madagascar. Like their Australian relatives, the Madagascar Rainbow likes slightly alkaline water. They spawn near the surface in fine-leaved plants, a few brown eggs a day. The eggs and fry are not usually eaten and will grow quickly on newly hatched brine shrimp. ◀

SHARKS AND LOACHES

Called "sharks" only because they bear a slight physical resemblance to the real sharks of the ocean, these bold little fellows are active, curious, and often mischievous. Most sharks need plenty of swimming space and will reward the keeper of a large tank with increased growth and more intense coloration.

If several of the same species are kept together, provide them with some retreats in the form of rocks, roots, and some tough aquarium plants.

▲ Leconte's Loach's (*Botia lecontei*) subdued coloration blossoms with good food and maturity. Don't overlook this classy fish in favor of its flashier cousins.

▼ Hora's Loach (*Botia morleti*) is a sweetheart that will grow to about four inches. If you remember that your loaches and sharks have downward-facing mouths, you will realize that they like to take their foods from the bottom of the aquarium.

►

The Orange-Finned Loach (*Botia modesta*) likes to have a place to hide when life becomes too stressful. A halved flowerpot or coconut shell will fill the bill.

◄ The Zebra Loach (*Botia striata*) is highly variable in pattern and color intensity. At times, the stripes are quite distinct with strong color contrast. In other specimens the bright color makes the stripes almost invisible.

The Bengal Loach (*Botia dario*). All of the *Botia* spp. are equipped with formidable switchblade-like spines under their eyes that pop out and lock in place when they are threatened. Any predator ▶ that tries to make a meal of a *Botia* is likely to be cutting its own throat.

◀ The Clown Loach (*Botia macracantha*) *is* a real clown with its gaudy colors, barrel-rolls, dips, dives, and leaps throughout the tank. After an exciting display of daredevilish piscine maneuvers, it will suddenly come to a dead stop as if exhausted by the performance. If you purchase a young Clown Loach, be sure to start it feeding with tubifex worms or you may lose your prize.

◀ The Red-Finned Shark (*Epalzeorhynchus frenatus*) is a hardy, fun-loving fish that is usually very long-lived in the aquarium. It will accept a wide range of water conditions, but has been spawned in slightly acid and moderately soft water.

The Tricolor or Bala Shark (*Balantiocheilos melanopterus*). Healthy and well fed Tricolor sharks can become rather large in the aquarium, although they are unlikely to reach the 10-inch size that is attained in nature. They are peaceful in comparison to many of the other "sharks" of the aquarium, but they are fast- ▲ swimming fish that need plenty of space.

◀ The Skunk Loach (*Botia sidthimunki*) at 1½ inches is the smallest of the *Botia* spp. and considered by many to be the best for the aquarium with its good looks and undemanding ways. Skunk loaches are very gregarious and like to be kept in schools.

Loaches are eel-like creatures that are natives of the muddy bottoms of places with romantic names like Sumatra, Borneo, Thailand, Malaysia, Burma, Java, etc. They are primarily nocturnal fishes, preferring to hide during the day and become active and feed in the hours of darkness.

They are built for access to tight places and have been known to travel up filter tubes into filters, where they delight in the tasty leftovers that have also landed in the filter.

▶ The pair wrap around each other and this stimulates the release of sperm and eggs. Some of the fertilized eggs float to the top of the water and some drop to the substrate.

▼ Shelford's Loach (*Pangio shelfordi*) is a native of Borneo. Loaches do best in soft, acid water and 75°F. They should be fed small foods (preferably live) that will sink to the bottom. They have no teeth, so it is important that the foods be small enough for them to eat.

The Weather Loach (*Misgurnus fossilis*) has the uncanny ability to predict storms. A Weather Loach is normally a sedate fish, but dropping barometric pressure (that indicates an approaching storm) causes it to dash wildly about the aquarium. ▼

▲ Prior to spawning, a pair of *Pangio myersi* start swimming about at the top of the water. The sexes are easy to determine in adult loaches. The female is significantly stouter around the middle.

▶ The male uses his barbels to grasp and hold the barbels of the female until he can get her into a position where spawning can take place.

◀ The Slimy Myersi (*Pangio myersi*) loves to hide under almost anything. Half of a coconut shell with a few holes in it, such as shown here, makes an ideal home.

ODDBALL ODYSSEY

Oddballs are fishes that have some unique characteristics—in their lifestyle, appearance, or behavior—that set them apart from the crowd. Some of the oddballs are set apart by the fact that they are a single species in a genus, some are "eccentrics" and hardly behave like fishes at all, and yet others have evolved in ways that will amuse (or astonish) us.

▲ The Red Snakehead (*Channa micropeltes*) is only a cute little red fish when it's a cute little young fish. When the Red Snakehead grows up, it can reach three feet in length, loses a lot of its attractive coloration, and has been known to attack small children in its native Indian waters!

▲ The Knight Goby (*Stigmatogobius sadanundio*) is a bottom-dwelling fish, as is usual for gobies. They require brackish water (about one tablespoon of salt for every two gallons) and must be fed live foods, especially worms and brine shrimp. Be sure to cover the aquarium securely; for bottom-dwellers, they sure are good jumpers!

▼ The Mudskipper (*Periophthalmus barbarus*) is a wonderful fish for an aquarium that is set up so there is an area of dry land. Mudskippers' powerful pectoral fins resemble short legs (or arms), that allow them to move over land very well. In fact, they do better on land than they do in the water and are clumsy swimmers. They require slightly brackish water.

◄ The Blind Cave Fish (*Amblyopsis spelaea*) lives in caves and has no eyes! Because of the lightless conditions in this fish's natural habitat, vision is unnecessary.

◄ The Scat (*Scatophagus argus*) is an estuarine fish that spends its time in coastal waters, so its water should be slightly salty. They are fond of live foods and should have some vegetable matter in their diets. Scats are very hardy, long-lived fish and primary players in most brackish aquaria.

▼ The Burmese Badis (*Badis badis burmanicus*) is an interesting little fish that acts like a dwarf cichlid (though it's not). They breed on rocks like the dwarf cichlids, but unlike the cichlids, the mother doesn't chase the father off after spawning. Both parents take care of the eggs and fry. They are peaceful and somewhat timid, so if you want to keep them happy, keep them with their own kind in a well-planted aquarium.

▼ The Desert Goby (*Chlamydogobious eremius*) is an Australian native that inhabits artesian springs and bores and accepts a wide range of water conditions. It is easy to feed in the aquarium, taking every kind of food with gratitude.

Knifefish, Flatfish, Leaffish, Butterflyfish, Elephantnose...all names that describe the oddballs. Some can breathe out of water, some fly, some walk, and some of them even swim! Many oddballs have special needs, so it is a good idea to read first, then prepare your tank, and only then buy your fish.

▲ The Leaffish (*Monocirrhus polyacanthus*) is so perfectly camouflaged, it looks exactly like a leaf as it waits patiently for its unsuspecting prey. In fact, the Leaffish even swims like a leaf, on its side.

▲ The Spiny Eel (*Mastacembalus armatus*) sleeps under the gravel! It is a nocturnal fish that likes its privacy and will spend its days nicely buried in the substrate. The rest of its time is spent digging around in the gravel for bits of food and tubifex worms.

▶ The Clown Knifefish (*Notopterus chitala*) is a big, nocturnal fish that needs a very large, heavily planted tank with dim lighting. A single specimen will live a long time in a quiet tank with a *lot* of live foods.

◀ The Butterflyfish (*Pantodon buchholzi*) flutters just under the surface of the water snapping up insects. Not a fish to let a tasty treat fly away, the Butterflyfish "takes off" and leaves the water with strong beats of its pectoral fins.

◀ The Freshwater Flounder (*Achirus lineatus*) is a quiet bottom-dwelling fish whose appetite for live tubifex will astound you. Give this fish a fine sand substrate as it likes to spend its time half-buried in the sand.

▲ The Climbing Perch (*Anabas testudineus*) is a native of swampy places in the Orient where, when its pool dries out, it waddles off in search of another body of water. They are very aggressive and should not be kept with other fishes.

The Marbled Eel (*Synbranchus marmoratus*) is perfect for the individual who likes a nasty fish with a big appetite that will scare off intruders. Many people think they are snakes when they first see them, but they are true eels. ▼

Peter's Elephantnose (*Gnathonemus petersi*) is an interesting African native that is peaceful and shy. It needs a gently lit, planted tank with small-sized gravel that will not damage its tender "nose." ▶

Many of the oddballs are unusual and not commonly found in pet shops. When you do run across an oddball in a dealer's tank, and you have an empty tank at home, consider buying it. You will enjoy learning about your unusual new fish and observing its unusual lifestyle.

▶ The Archerfish (*Toxotes jaculator*) knocks its prey right out of the air by spitting a perfectly aimed jet of water.

The Congo Puffer (*Tetraodon miurus*) looks like a potato! Its body colors are capable of considerable change and it matches its surroundings quite easily. It often burrows into the bottom with only its eyes showing, waiting for its prey. ▶

▼ The Sleeper Goby (*Hypseleotris compressa*) is a native of "Down Under." A favorite find, it will eat just about anything and earns its place in the aquarium for its beautiful colors alone.

Somphongs' Puffer (*Carinotetraodon somphongsi*) will rid a tank of snails in no time flat. It has sharp little teeth and strong jaws, but is somewhat more peaceful towards other fish than many of the puffers. ▶

▲ The Brazilian Freshwater Puffer (*Colomesus asellus*) is a river fish that is happy in fresh or slightly brackish water. They are fond of snails but will eat large live foods and strips of fish.

▲
The puffer's claim to fame is its full-blown defense mechanism. Puffers will inflate at the first sign of danger, appearing larger than they are and hopefully preventing predators from swallowing them. After the danger has passed, they deflate and return to normal size.

▼ The African Whale (*Petrocephalus simus*) prefers a dimly lit aquarium where it can have some privacy from time to time. An aquarium favorite for its peaceful temperament, it will eat small worms, brine shrimp, and daphnia, but never bothers its tankmates.

▼ The Bumblebee Goby (*Brachygobius doriae*) is a brackish water fish that will not live long in an aquarium without salt. The best way to keep them is in a small aquarium by themselves, where you can enjoy them hopping around the bottom looking for brine shrimp.

INDEX - COMMON NAMES